Scampers
Thinks Like a Scientist

By Mike Allegra ~ Illustrated by Elizabeth Zechel

Dawn Publications

Dedications

For the classroom teachers in my family: my wife, mom, dad, sister, and father-in-law. — MA

For Charlie. — EZ

Library of Congress Cataloging-in-Publication Data
Names: Allegra, Mike, author. | Zechel, Elizabeth, illustrator.
Title: Scampers thinks like a scientist/ by Mike Allegra ; illustrated by
  Elizabeth Zechel.
Description: First edition. | Nevada City, CA : Dawn Publications, [2019] |
  Audience: Ages 3-8. | Audience: K to grade 3.
Identifiers: LCCN 2018026280| ISBN 9781584696421 (hardback) | ISBN
  9781584696438 (pbk.)
Subjects: LCSH: Science--Methodology--Juvenile literature. |
  Science--Experiments--Juvenile literature. | Mice--Juvenile literature.
Classification: LCC Q175.2 .A45 2019 | DDC 507.2/1--dc23
LC record available at https://lccn.loc.gov/2018026280

Book design and computer production by Patty Arnold, *Menagerie Design & Publishing*

Manufactured by Regent Publishing Services, Hong Kong

Printed January, 2019, in ShenZhen, Guangdong, China

10 9 8 7 6 5 4 3 2 1

First Edition

Dawn Publications

12402 Bitney Springs Road
Nevada City, CA 95959
www.dawnpub.com

The vegetable garden was the place to be.

It was where every mouse in the valley went
to chat and dance and laugh and play.

To see and be seen...and,
of course, to eat!

Until the owl arrived.

The miserable mice found some food in the distant fields, but not nearly enough. Still, they all agreed that having a hungry belly was better than filling the belly of a hungry owl.

So they stayed far, far away.

Except for Scampers.

She hid in the weeds outside of
The vegetable garden and
watched the owl all day
and all night.

She kept very still. The owl kept still,
too. *Very* still. Maybe a bit *too* still.

"Why doesn't the owl move?"
Scampers wondered.

In the morning, her friend Nibbles crept up beside her. "What are you doing here? That thing will eat you!"

"Maybe," Scampers said. "But maybe not."

"Maybe *not*?" asked Nibbles.

"Maybe we should find out," Scampers replied. "Let's get to work."

The next day, they brought a rag-doll mouse
into the garden. It bobbed this way and that.

Skippita skippita skippta.

It hopped onto a head of cauliflower.

Skippita skippita skippta.

And it danced a mousy mambo.

"The owl is not flying," Scampers said. "The owl is not eating."

"Maybe owls can tell if a mouse is fake," Nibbles whispered.

"Then maybe we need a *real* mouse," suggested Scampers.

"Maybe we don't!" said Nibbles.

But Scampers had already leapt from her hiding place.

HELLO!

"Shh! It might hear us,"
Nibbles hissed.

"THAT'S THE IDEA!"
she bellowed.
"BUT IT'S *NOT*
HEARING US!"

"Maybe owls are
hard of hearing,"
he murmured.

TWEEDLE-DEEDLE! CRASH!

"Maybe owls are *very* hard of hearing," Nibbles wondered.

"Then maybe we should be more obvious," Scampers declared.

Nibbles gulped, "Maybe *more* obvious?!"

"It took a while, but I invented something more obvious," Scampers explained. "This is an eggapult. And this is an egg in my eggapult."

KA-TWANG! sPLAT!

The owl didn't move.
"Maybe owls don't mind eggs?"
Nibbles offered.

So Scampers tried a rock.

KA-TWANG! CLUNK!

The owl didn't move.
"Maybe owls...
have hard heads?"
Nibbles suggested.

"Maybe we should figure out all of your maybes,"
Scampers smiled. "Maybe we should try this stuff out
on another owl. And the best place to find one is in the woods!"

"*Definitely* not!" cried Nibbles.

No no no no no! NOOOOOOOOOOOOO!

Scampers found the perfect spot.

"Ready?" she asked.

"No," Nibbles said.

But Scampers yelled anyway.

HELLO!

An owl's head spun around.

Scampers poked the rag doll out from
their hiding place.

skippita skippita – SNAP!

The doll disappeared.

Then Scampers egg-a-pulted a rock.

KA-TWANG! BONK!

SKWAAAK!

"Maybe…" Nibbles began.

"Maybe what?" interrupted Scampers.

"Maybe you've figured out why the garden owl doesn't move," he grinned.

The next day, Scampers made a poster to show the other mice
what she and Nibbles had discovered.

"Maybe you're using too much glitter," suggested Nibbles.

"Maybe I need *more!*" Scampers squealed.

Then she called a Meeting of the Mice.

"Nibbles and I have been studying owls,"
Scampers announced to her audience.
"Owls move. Owls fly. Owls eat mice."

A mouse shouted,
we know that!

"But the vegetable garden owl didn't move,
fly, eat, or SKWAAAK!" explained Scampers.

"So what?" another mouse asked.

"So the vegetable garden owl is a fake owl!" Nibbles cried.

"We have nothing to fear!" Scampers declared.
"Our garden is unguarded! Let's go!"

Scampers leapt from the mouse nest, raced across the field,
and didn't stop until she reached the garden gate.
She shoved it open and turned to welcome everyone inside.

But no one was there except Nibbles.

"They still don't believe you," he said.

"Well, sometimes a new discovery is so amazing
    that others need a little time to accept it," Scampers replied.

  "So while they're thinking it over,
      let's eat."

Explore More for Kids

Thinking Like a Scientist

When the owl arrived in the garden, most of the mice ran away. But not Scampers. She started thinking like a scientist to understand the situation.

Scientists ask questions.

Scampers was curious about the owl. She watched it day and night and noticed something unusual. She wondered, "Why doesn't the owl move?"

Scientists investigate.

Scampers tried many different things to get the owl in the garden to move. Then she tried those same things with the owl in the woods.

As part of her investigation, Scampers also had to **think like an engineer**. Engineers use tools to help them solve problems. Scampers designed and created a rag-doll mouse and an eggapult.

Scientists construct explanations.

Scampers compared the behavior of the garden owl to the behavior of a forest owl. Based on her observations, she had an explanation for why the garden owl didn't move. It was a fake owl!

Scientists communicate information.

Scampers and Nibbles presented a poster and showed the results of their investigation to the other mice. They explained why and how they knew that the garden owl was a fake owl.

Really? I Don't Believe It!

The other mice didn't believe that the garden owl was a fake. But Scampers knew that sometimes a new discovery is so amazing that others need a little time to accept it.

More About...

The OWL

The real owl in the story is a Great Horned Owl. The mice had good reason to be terrified of this owl. It will eat several mice a night, swallowing them whole.

Great Horned Owls are built for hunting. They can surprise their prey because they fly quietly. They swoop in to grab their prey with sharp talons (claws).

Great Horned Owls don't really have horns—just tufts of feathers on their heads. They can turn their heads to look behind and pinpoint a mouse in the weeds in the dark.

The mice easily noticed the owl in the garden because it was meant to be seen. Many gardeners put a fake owl on top of a post or roof to scare away mice and other animals that eat crops.

MICE

The mice in this story are field mice. They are food for owls and many other animals. Mice are mostly active at night (nocturnal). Darkness hides them from most predators, but not from owls.

Mice are fantastic engineers. They create underground burrows designed with specific "rooms" to store food, sleep, and poop. Burrows are usually close to a good food source.

Mice can squeeze into the tightest of spaces. If their heads can fit through a hole, so can the rest of their bodies. The hole only needs to be the size of a dime.

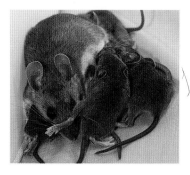

Mice only live about six months in the wild. Mice make up for their short lifespan by having very large families. In captivity, a mouse can live for several years.

Literacy Connection—Read Aloud Suggestions

1. Preview the book ahead of time. There is a lot of dialogue between the main characters Scampers and Nibbles. Practice reading with expression to emphasize the different personality of each character to bring out the humor.

2. Read the title and identify the author and illustrator. Explain what each one does. Examine the cover illustration. Ask *Who is Scampers? What is happening in the illustration? How does it relate to the title?* Ask children to make predictions of what the book is about.

3. As you read the story, pause occasionally to have children make predictions by asking *What do you think Scampers is going to do next?"*

4. Have children review their predictions by asking *What is the book about? What information does the author give you?*

5. Discuss what a scientist does. Read the book again, identifying how Scampers is using scientific processes.

6. Read aloud the "Explore More for Kids" section, continuing your discussion about scientific processes and learning information about owls and mice.

7. Discuss some of the scientific discoveries that people didn't believe at first, for example: the earth is round and the earth revolves around the sun.

Science and Engineering Practices

Science and Engineering Practices (NGSS)	Classroom Applications Exemplified by Scampers
Asking Questions (for science) and Defining Problems (for engineering)	• Ask questions based on observations to find out more information about the natural world. • Ask questions that can be answered by an investigation.
Planning and Carrying Out Investigations	• Conduct an investigation to produce data to serve as the basis for evidence to answer a question. • Make observations to collect data that can be used to make comparisons.
Analyzing and Interpreting Data	• Use and share pictures or drawings of observations. • Use observations to describe patterns and relationships in the natural world in order to answer scientific questions.
Constructing Explanations and Designing Solutions	• Make observations to construct an evidence-based account for natural phenomena. • Use evidence (observations, patterns) to support an explanation.
Engaging in Argument from Evidence	• Distinguish between opinions and evidence in one's own explanations. • Construct an argument with evidence to support a claim.
Obtaining, Evaluating, and Communicating Information	• Communicate information with others in oral forms, using drawings to provide detail about scientific ideas.

STEM Activities

The four components of STEM (Science, Technology, Engineering, and Math) are included in the Scientific and Engineering processes. The following activities may be used alone or as part of a comprehensive lesson.

Science

The garden is a great place for conducting outdoor experiments. If you can't get outside, you can do this experiment inside. Begin with the question: What conditions will grow the tallest plants? Divide students into small groups and have them design an experiment that tests just one of the following growing conditions (variables):

- Three different amounts of light

- Three different amounts of water

- Three different kinds of soil, such as sand, clay, garden potting soil, or dirt from the school grounds

Give each group three pots, seeds, tape, and markers (for labeling the pots), and data sheets for recording their conditions and plant measurements. Have groups predict what they think will happen for each condition. Allow several weeks for students to regularly measure the plants' growth. Conclude by having each group create a poster showing their results and identifying the best conditions for growing healthy plants. Based on the results, can the class answer the original question (What conditions will grow the tallest plants?) or do they need to do additional experiments?

Technology

Seeing an owl is a thrilling experience! And with the aid of technology (wild bird cams) people everywhere can watch the inside of owl nests online. Cornell Lab of Ornithology and Audubon bird cams are a good source for owl cams, as well as cams for several other kinds of birds: http://cams.allaboutbirds.org/all-cams/ and https://www.audubon.org/birdcams.

Engineering

Scampers used engineering skills to design her "eggapult." Although tossing eggs and rocks through the air is dangerous, tossing pompoms with a popsicle catapult is safe. For each

catapult, you'll need 6 craft sticks, 6 rubber bands, one plastic spoon, and several pompoms. For complete directions go to https://buggyandbuddy.com/stem-activity-for-kids-popsicle-stick-catapults/ or refer to *The Curious Kid's Science Book* by Asia Citro.

Have students measure how far their catapult tossed a pompom. Then have them alter the design of the catapult (moving the spoon, using more or less rubber bands, or another modification) to try to gain more distance. Compare their results and identify the design that threw the pompoms the farthest. Compare students' designs with Scamper's eggapult. Which one do they think would work the best? Why?

Math

Math skills are incorporated directly into the science and engineering activities (above) as students measure the height of their plants and the distance their catapults threw the pompoms. You may also have students create bar graphs comparing heights or distances.

There are many useful resources online for most of Dawn's books, including **activities**, **bookmarks**, and **standards-based lesson plans**. Scan this code to go directly to resources for this book, or go to www.dawnpub.com and click on "Activities" for this and other books.

Mike Allegra is the author of *Sarah Gives Thanks*, *Everybody's Favorite Book*, and the *Prince Not-So Charming* chapter book series (pen name: Roy L. Hinuss). This is Mike's first book with Dawn Publications. He was the winner of the 2014 *Highlights* Fiction Contest and a recipient of an Individual Artist Fellowship from the New Jersey State Council for the Arts. Mike also has a great affection for rodents; he has cared for mice, a three-legged gerbil, one fancy rat, one sewer rat masquerading as a fancy rat, and the world's most ornery guinea pig. Stop by his blog at www.mikeallegra.com and say hello!

Elizabeth Zechel is an illustrator and author of the children's book *Is There a Mouse in the Baby's Room?* Other picture books she's illustrated include the *Lucy's Lab* series of books by Michelle Houts, *Wordbirds: An Irreverent Lexicon for the 21st Century* by Liesl Schillinger, and *The Little General and the Giant Snowflake* by Matthea Harvey. She has also illustrated a cookbook, *Bubby's Homemade Pies*, by Jen Bervin and Ron Silver, and contributes illustrations to various magazine and literary journals. This is Elizabeth's first book for Dawn Publications. Elizabeth lives in Brooklyn where she teaches kindergarten.

More Science and Nature Books from Dawn Publications

The Mouse and the Meadow—A curious young mouse (not Scampers) boldly ventures into the meadow for the first time. Science and story blend seamlessly together.

Paddle Perch Climb: Bird Feet Are Neat—Lively paper collages and a rhythmic text have kids guessing what bird will be revealed. Gentle lessons and a few surprises!

Daytime Nighttime, All Through the Year—Delightful rhymes and unique illustrations depict two animals for each month, one active during the day and one busy at night.

Pitter and Patter—Follow along with two drops of rain as they make their way through the water cycle, meeting a fascinating array of critters on their journey.

In the Trees, Honey Bees—Readers get an inside-the-hive view of a wild colony, along with solid information about these remarkable and valuable creatures.

A Moon of My Own—An imaginative young girl journeys around the world, accompanied by her faithful companion—the Moon. As her travels progress, the phases of the moon change.

Tall Tall Tree—Discover the animals that make their home in a tall, tall tree—a magnificent coast redwood. Rhyming verses and a 1-10 counting scheme make this a real page-turner.

Over in the Forest: Come and Take a Peek—Children learn the ways of forest animals to the rhythm of the traditional tune "Over in a Meadow." This book is part of the award-winning series that includes biomes and locations from around the world: ocean, rainforest, river, mountain, desert, arctic, grasslands, and Australia.

Dawn Publications is dedicated to inspiring in children a deeper understanding and appreciation for all life on Earth. You can browse through our titles, download resources for teachers, and order at www.dawnpub.com or call 800-545-7475.